KALPANA CHAWLA

Born to a traditional family in Karnal, Haryana, Kalpana Chawla was the youngest of four children. She fought odds and overcame obstacles to pursue aeronautical engineering from Punjab Engineering College and then went abroad to earn a doctorate in aerospace engineering from the University of Colorado, USA.

She joined NASA, where she was described as a 'terrific engineer'. Soon, she was selected as an astronaut candidate. She made the journey into space not once but twice. Her promising life ended tragically during her second tour to space, when the space shuttle *Columbia* disintegrated on February 1, 2003.

Even through her short life, she inspired many around the world to follow their dreams and passion.

KALPANA CHAWLA

INDIA'S FIRST WOMAN ASTRONAUT

Dilip M Salwi

Published by
Rupa Publications India Pvt. Ltd 2004, 2016
161-B/4, Gulmohar House,
Yusuf Sarai Community Centre,
New Delhi 110049

Sales centres:
Bengaluru Chennai
Hyderabad Kolkata Mumbai

P-ISBN-978-81-291-3091-4
E-ISBN-978-81-291-4084-5

Eighth impression 2026

10 9 8

Printed in India

To my loving daughter,
Neha Salwi, the 'Supergirl'

CONTENTS

CHAPTER I

CELEBRATIONS TURN INTO MOURNING

For a fortnight they had orbited the earth at an altitude of 360 kilometres in space at the hypersonic speed of 26,000 kilometres per hour and conducted several scientific experiments successfully. Now, Commander Rick Husband turned around the huge aeroplane-like, black and white tile-covered Space Shuttle *Columbia* by firing its smaller, thruster jets for the return journey to earth. It was 8 o'clock on the morning of February 1, 2003. From their vantage point in space, they could see the huge, bluish Indian Ocean covered with whitish wisps of clouds right below them. Their destination—the runaway near Cape Canaveral of the Kennedy Space Centre, about 50 minutes away—was on the other side of the earth. With the shuttle's tail pointing toward the earth, the Commander frequently fired its main engines like brakes, to reduce its orbiting speed so that the shuttle descended slowly into the thin, upper terrestrial atmosphere.

Meanwhile, the five other astronauts aboard the shuttle had packed their bags and strapped themselves to their seats, cracking jokes and exchanging smiles, eagerly awaiting their landing on earth. The moment of meeting their families—all gathered at the Kennedy Space Centre to view the touchdown—seemed not too far away. Shortly, after firing its thruster jets for manoeuvring, the shuttle started descending like a glider through the atmosphere, which grew denser with the falling altitude. The friction of its huge body against the denser atmosphere produced tremendous heat. Consequently, the temperature rose very fast as the shuttle descended through the atmosphere.

From the windows next to their seats the astronauts could see nothing but a pinkish haze of heat that had engulfed their shuttle. Soon, it began to descend in a series of S-turns and flew over the islands of Hawaii in the Pacific Ocean below. All the radio links with Mission Control at Houston, USA, were cut off as the heat haze—rising to temperatures as high as 1,700 degree Celsius—turned the surrounding air into a blanket of electrically charged particles that shut off all radio waves.

Radio contact with Mission Control was resumed fifteen minutes later when the shuttle was cruising at an altitude of 63 kilometres, with its nose tilted at a 40-degree angle exposing only its belly to the raging atmospheric heat. The shuttle was then gliding over San Francisco Bay and was hardly sixteen minutes away from its scheduled landing at Kennedy Space Centre's runaway. At that very moment, the sensors aboard the twenty-three-year old shuttle indicated to Mission Control some temperature anomalies over its left wing and also a reduction of pressure in one of its tyres.

The seven member crew of the Space Shuttle Columbia. Kalpana Chawla is seated fourth from left.

However, before Mission Control could issue a warning to the Commander, the shuttle was engulfed in a ball of fire. Two loud booming sounds were heard as the orangish yellow ball of the shuttle split apart across the early morning blue sky of Texas. Shortly, the two glittering points of light broke into more shining fragments as they glided down to fall like a hot hailstorm over a huge region of Texas and its neighbouring states. In less than five minutes, the shuttle had broken into more than a thousand pieces and all the seven astronauts aboard were dead in mid-air. For the first time in the history of spaceflight, a spacecraft had met with such a tragic end while landing back on earth.

While the shuttle was approaching the earth with perfect weather landing conditions at Cape Canaveral at the scheduled time of 9:16 A.M., several thousands of kilometres away—on the other side of the earth—the wintery night had already set in over the small town of Karnal. The town is about 126 kilometres away from Delhi on the famous Grand Trunk Road and is named after Karna, one of the unforgettable heroes of the Indian epic the *Mahabharata.* That afternoon, the students of Tagore Baal Niketan Senior Secondary School had begun celebrating a historic event in their new school premises. The event was the return of a former student from a space flight for the second time. A few years ago, in 1998, the same student had become the first Indian woman astronaut to go into space. Overnight, she had become a national heroine. Moreover, she had not forgotten her alma mater and made provision for the yearly training of a few selected students from her school in space science and technology in the United States. Everyone was looking forward to her promised visit to the school after her return from space.

To celebrate her second space flight, the new building of the school was illuminated with multicoloured lights and students were singing and dancing the *bhangra* to the beat of drums. Fireworks were also kept ready for a colourful display at night. While people from the neighourhood gathered outside the school to watch them, a few reporters from a popular TV news channel also arrived and began to record the celebrations. Meanwhile, some students were eagerly watching the television for news of the safe landing of the shuttle. Then everyone fell silent as the news of the disaster of the *Columbia* started trickling in over the television channels.

As they all watched in shock, the news channels began to report that it was still not clear whether the astronauts were dead or alive. Hoping against hope they all rushed to the small shrine of the goddess Saraswati inside the school and began to pray for the safety of

Fiery end of Columbia

their former student. Other former students began to arrive to join in the prayers. Finally, late in the night, news channels reported that all the astronauts were dead and everybody broke down.

Rarely does a happy event to mark a historic occasion turn into a moment of grievous tragedy for an entire nation. Next morning India mourned the sudden loss of her first woman astronaut. She was Kalpana Chawla, the popular Kalpana Didi at her school. Her cometary rise from an obscure little town to enter the space programme is a heroic achievement for any Indian woman. Moreover, unlike India's first man in space, Rakesh Sharma, who went on a Russian spacecraft as an international passenger, Kalpana was a fully qualified career astronaut with important mission responsibilities.

Kalpana's life is an example of courage, conviction and determination and shows what an Indian woman can achieve given freedom and opportunities. A 'trail-blazer' in the true sense of the word, she has today become a symbol of courage and adventure. Had she lived on—who knows?—she could even have become the first woman to land on Mars, as scientists are planning to set up a base on that planet!

US President, George Bush at the memorial service held at Johnson Space Center, Houston

President George Bush of the United States said, 'None of our astronauts travelled a longer path to space than Kalpana Chawla,' while paying glowing tributes to the seven *Columbia* astronauts. People from every corner of India paid rich tributes to her as several awards, honours and scholarships were instituted in her memory. Poems were written glorifying her grit and determination and her death amongst the stars. But the greatest tribute was paid by the Indian Prime Minister, Atal Bihari Vajpayee when he re-named the latest *Metsat-1 as Kalpana-1*. It is the first in the series of Indian meteorological satellites launched into space on September 12, 2002 by an Indian rocket.

The memory of Kalpana would now be forever associated with space and stars. That is the place she wanted to conquer, and that is where she has found her final rest.

The Washington Post

'Columbia Is Lost'

Shuttle Disintegrates on Reentry, Killing 7 Aboard

CHAPTER II

AIMING FOR THE SKY

Kalpana's parents originally came to Karnal from the Multan district of West Punjab (now Pakistan) after the Partition. When her father, Banarsi Lal Chawla, was leaving his hometown of Sheikhopura, communal riots broke out. He was one of the few survivors in the family who managed to reach India safely but without any possessions. The family finally settled down in Karnal, Haryana. Even today, his parents and brother are remembered in that small town for their services to the poor and needy.

For his own survival, Kalpana's father started several petty businesses, from selling toffees, groundnuts, dates and soaps as a street hawker to fabricating metal boxes for storing provisions and even setting up a textile shop. Finally, he became a self-taught technologist and engineer and began manufacturing tyres when the Indian market was flooded with imported tyres. Meanwhile, he married Sanyogita, a highly religious young woman, whose family also came from the same region in Pakistan. His is the proverbial rags-to-riches story and today he owns a flourishing tyre manufacturing company which has spread its wings all over the world.

When Kalpana was born on March 17, 1962, in Karnal, her father was still a petty businessman trying hard to support his growing joint family of sixteen members. Kalpana was brought up in an environment where hard work was encouraged. The youngest child among three girls and one boy, she was treated like any other girl in the family, expected to be obedient and docile. But Kalpana's mother came from an educated family and was always ready to fight for her daughters. In fact, by the time Kalpana grew up, her eldest sister Sunita, eight years her senior, had already broken several family traditions. She had done well in school and gone for higher education to college, which was a taboo for girls in those days.

Even as a child, Kalpana began to show her independent nature and she even selected own name! It so happened that she was called by her pet name 'Monto' at home. Her parents were always so busy that

Kalpana during her school days

Kalpana had not been formally named at a proper ceremony. When Sunita and her aunt took Kalpana for admission to a nearby nursery school, the Principal asked her name. 'We have three names in mind—Kalpana, Jyotsna and Sunaina, but we haven't decided...,' replied Sunita. The Principal therefore asked the little girl 'Which name do you like?' And she replied firmly, 'Kalpana...!'

Like the name she chose, which means 'imagination', Kalpana was a highly imaginative child. During summer when the family slept on the roof of their small house in an isolated corner of Model Town colony, she would watch the night sky. Staring at the twinkling stars she wondered what they were, dreaming they beckoned to her and if it was ever possible to reach them. She would often ask questions about space but would rarely receive a satisfactory answer. Stars captivated her so much that once when she and her classmates built a physical geography map of India covering the floor of an entire classroom in her school, Tagore Baal Niketan, she covered its ceiling completely with stars—sparkling dots marked on blackened newspapers!

Like stars in the night sky, the first things in the blue morning sky that caught her fancy were aeroplanes. Karnal is one of the few Indian towns with a flying club. It was called 'Karnal Aviation Club' and is now a part of the Haryana Institute of Civil Aviation. Here, small *Pushpak* planes and gliders regularly take off and land. As her house was a few kilometres away from the Club, her favourite pastime was to climb up to the roof and watch them go roaring over her head. Bewitched, she would wave her hand at the pilot if the plane flew low over the house.

Karnal Aviation Club

Whenever her teachers asked her class to draw a scenery, she would always draw aeroplanes flying in the sky, while the rest made mountains, rivers and houses. She also loved making models of aeroplanes during craft classes.

Once during a class, she asked her teacher Daljit K. Madan whether she had ever flown in an aeroplane. When she said no, Kalpana enquired whether she was afraid of flying. At the age of eleven, she persuaded her father to take her to the Club and had a thrilling joyride aboard a *Pushpak*. From that day on, flying became her first love. She became as excited as a child whenever she saw planes or talked about them. And, one of the questions this inquisitive and sensitive girl asked after

The new premises of Tagore Baal Niketan (inset) A group photograph of Kalpana with her classmates and two of her favourite teachers, Nirmala Namboodiripad and Daljit K. Madaan

the joyride was, how can people be divided into classes, sects and religions, when they all look alike from the sky?

Although Kalpana never scored the highest marks in her class she was always among the first five. Sincere, hard-working and attentive, she respected and admired her teachers. She enjoyed subjects like English, Hindi and geography but her favourite subject was science taught by Nirmala Namboodripad, who took pains to make the subject simple and interesting. Kalpana also wrote poetry and danced at the annual day celebrations. She loved cycling and running and at sports meets she always came first in the races. Friendly and helpful, she often played badminton and dodge ball with boys. As she grew into a young woman, she cut her hair short and never put on any make-up. She refused to cook,

DAV College for Women, Karnal

never ironed her clothes, and began to wear trousers or jeans. During her elder sister's marriage, she wore the same dress for three days, saying that it did not matter what you wear!

In those days, most girls in Karnal completed their education, got married and settled down. But her teachers at school encouraged the girls not to waste their education and do something more worthwhile in life. Belonging to middle or lower middle class families, the girls were also keen on higher studies and earning a living. By the tenth class, Kalpana had also made up her mind. Whenever any visitor asked her what she wanted to become in life, she would promptly reply, 'A Flight Engineer!' She thought that a flight engineer designs aeroplanes as nobody had explained that a flight engineer navigates an aeroplane during its flight! Once she saw a photograph of the *Viking* lander on the planet Mars in a popular weekly and her imaginative mind woke up to the possibility of travelling in space and landing on the Red Planet.

Dyal Singh College

Like her elder sisters she was admitted to an exclusive girls college—DAV College for Women for her Pre-University. She passed her 10th class from the Haryana Board Examination in 1976. Actually, she was underage and got away by changing her date of birth from March 17, 1962 to July 1, 1961.

Teachers at the DAV College encouraged her interest in science and mathematics and urged her to go for higher studies. There was a prophetic incident during a mathematics class. The teacher, Swarn Arora, was teaching what is called a 'Null set' or empty set in modern algebra. Giving the example of this set, she said that an Indian woman astronaut was the classic case as till then no Indian woman had become an astronaut. To the surprise of everybody, Kalpana instantly exclaimed, 'Who knows, Madam, one day this set may not exist?' At that

Punjab Engineering College, Chandigarh

juncture, nobody in the class could imagine that one day she herself would fill the set!

After successfully completing Pre-University, Kalpana realised that she would have to shift to the neighbouring co-ed Dyal Singh College, if she wanted to pursue her dream of an engineering career. Nobody had told her earlier that it was the only college in Karnal that offered the Pre-Engineering course required for admission to an engineering college. Fortunately, it was not too late. She joined Dyal Singh College for the Pre-Engineering course, passed it with excellence and secured admission in the Punjab Engineering College, Chandigarh.

It was after Kalpana had secured admission to the Punjab Engineering College that her father, whose business often kept him out of Karnal, became aware of her plans and tried his best to dissuade her. He felt, a girl had no career prospects in engineering and advised her to become a doctor or a school teacher. He was not against her going to Chandigarh because earlier, Sunita had done her higher studies there but Kalpana was adamant. She was determined to become a flight engineer and for that, an engineering degree was essential.

Although her father was conservative by temperament, he always gave in when he realised that Kalpana had made up her mind. Moreover, her mother and eldest sister always firmly supported her. That Kalpana had already secured admission in the engineering college was a strong argument in her favour. So, after much discussion in the family, her father finally gave in, but he was too busy to accompany her to Chandigarh. To give her moral support, her mother accompanied Kalpana to Chandigarh instead. Her father's objections were not unreasonable, a girl aiming for an engineering career was a rarity in those days.

Then to top it all, Kalpana opted for the aeronautical engineering course. Of the seven girls who joined that year, she was the only one to do so. Asked during her admission what was her second option, she replied that she had none! During counselling for the selection of various engineering courses, the teachers also tried to dissuade her from opting for aeronautic engineering as it had limited job opportunities in the country. They tried to shift her to electrical engineering which other girls had joined but she refused to budge. Nobody could change her mind. She was determined to become a flight engineer, and nothing on earth could stop her!

In college, Kalpana showed total dedication to her subject because she enjoyed what she was doing. In fact, she was always dissatisfied with her performance and felt she could have done better. Always dressed in trousers, she used to come to college on a bicycle. As there was no girl's hostel, initially she stayed in Mata Gujri Hall in the Punjab University campus. In fact, she changed several hostels as she found the hostel environment very noisy and distracting for studies. Later, she lived alone in one room above a garage in a bungalow.

Kalpana had a few select friends and would restrict herself to them and her studies. She learnt karate and became a black belt. She was mentally prepared to fight if any man tried to act smart with her. She also had an aesthetic sense in clothes, was fond of eating simple food and collecting precious stones. She loved a quiet environment and reading books. During those days, her favourite writers were Ayn Rand, Alexander Solzhenitsyn, Salman Rushdie, Richard Bach and Oriana Fallaci. She would even persuade other friends to read these writers. Besides helping her friends in studies, she regularly paid the fees of one poor batchmate out of her pocket money without the girl's knowledge. Although she believed herself to be no less than any boy and could do any task that they could, she disliked the more aggressive women's liberation movement of the West.

Kalpana always kept herself informed of developments in the world of aviation. She collected books and magazines on the subject and read them from cover to cover. She was particularly fond of Kelly Johnson's book on designing high-tech aeroplanes under a cloak of secrecy in the United States. Throughout her aeronautical studies at the sprawling campus of the college, she took an active part in various extra-curricular activities, which eventually helped in her selection to an American university. In the first year she wrote for the college magazine 'PECMAG' on precious stones and in the subsequent years she was its student editor. In the same year at the Annual Colloquium, she surprised her seniors by presenting a paper on 'Time-lapse in Space' dealing with Albert Einstein's Theories of Relativity.

Kalpana during a seminar at the Punjab Engineering College, Chandigarh

Kalpana also became the Joint Secretary of the Aero and Astro Club of the college. Under its auspices, she arranged several lectures and seminars on issues, such as, the role of women in society, the political scenario in the subcontinent, etc. She also conducted several quiz competitions. Once she arranged for the showing of the film *Those Magnificent Men in Their Flying Machines* to her classmates when she came to know that they had not seen it. She was one of the few students who was interested in aero-modelling and regularly visited parks near the college to fly aero-models with her classmate R K Jolly. She also took part in college sports meets, participating in running, cycling and rope-skipping races.

Always forthright in her manners and ready to take a stand on important issues, Kalpana won the respect of her classmates. If ever the question of a future career was discussed she would always point to the sky and say, 'I'm going to fly!' Sometimes, friends teased her for her passion for flying. Kalpana was respectful and courteous to all her teachers and was always keen to learn any new thing from anybody, be it a clerical job or handling a sophisticated equipment. She had a special regard for two professors in the Aeronautical Engineering Division, namely V S Malhotra and S C Sharma, who always encouraged and supported her. Her teachers found that while most of the students were only keen on good grades and securing a degree, she always enjoyed understanding things and working on new projects.

In 1982, Kalpana secured the third position in her class when she passed the BSc (Engineering) degree.

By virtue of being the only woman candidate, she also became the first woman aeronautical engineer of the college. Despite all the hurdles in her path, she had managed to stick to her first love and was then fully qualified to design aeroplanes. This was, however, just the first step to much greater heights that she would achieve in the years ahead.

CHAPTER III

FROM SKY TO SPACE

While Kalpana was in her final year at the engineering college, she began preparations to join an American university for higher studies. After graduation she had got job offers from some organisations, such as Hindustan Aeronautics Limited, Bangalore. But she opted for a teaching assignment at the Punjab Engineering College only because she felt it could be used as a stop-gap arrangement before she secured admission in the United States. She was keen to study more about her subject before taking up a job.

Meanwhile, her father's new enterprise in tyre manufacturing was flourishing and the tyres were being exported abroad. He was often away from Karnal and was keen that his children should take care of the business in his absence. Her elder brother Sanjay had already joined him and Kalpana feared that one day she would also be coaxed into joining it. She therefore did not return to Karnal even for a short break after completing her BSc degree.

Soon, Kalpana was offered admission in some US universities but the course she preferred was in the Department of Aerospace Science and Engineering in the University of Texas at Arlington. Moreover, the Department also offered her financial assistance which she needed badly. But the last date of joining the university was not very far away and her father was still abroad. Without his approval and assistance, she could not leave.

Fortunately, her father returned home just a few weeks before the last date of admission. When he came to know that she was teaching at Chandigarh and had also secured admission to an American university, he was very upset. He went to Chandigarh planning to bring the recalcitrant girl back home. He first met the Principal of the college to find out her whereabouts. When the Principal came to know that he was Kalpana's father, he took him to task for being too busy and ignoring her talent. Then the Principal convinced him that future opportunities in her specialised subject of aeronautics lay only in the United States.

As her father neared the room where Kalpana was taking a senior engineering class, he caught a glimpse of her through a side window. And his heart filled with pride, seeing his 'little' daughter teaching engineering to senior boys. When Kalpana saw her father outside the classroom, she immediately came out to the corridor and told him angrily that she had missed a golden opportunity of studying abroad due to his delay in returning home. To her great surprise, he assured her that she would join the same year and in time if that was her wish! He even asked her to resign from her job immediately and return to Karnal to prepare for her journey. For a moment, Kalpana thought he was trying to trick her into returning home. But his subsequent actions convinced her of his genuine concern. In the next

few days, he literally ran from pillar to post to get her passport issued, her ticket booked and visa okayed. He also booked his son's ticket to the US so that he could escort her to the university and ensure that she was well settled there. Through his contacts in the US, the university even made a special arrangement to pick her up at the airport and admit her even when the last date was over!

Within a few hours of reaching the University of Texas at Arlington, Kalpana met her future husband, the six-footer, broad shouldered Jean Pierre Harrison, who lived a few rows away from her apartment. A Frenchman who had taken US citizenship, he was popularly known as 'JP' and was a freelance flying instructor in the local flying club. Flying being her first love too, a friendship grew as she realised that they shared many interests like listening to music, reading and hiking. Within a year she felt she had met her life partner and despite initial protests by family members, she married Harrison at a simple ceremony on December 2, 1983. But she retained her maiden name - shortened to 'KC' by friends who found it hard to pronounce her name. Later, Kalpana also became a citizen of the United States.

But till the end of her life Kalpana did not lose touch with her roots. She mixed with the Indian community

Kalpana with her French American husband Jean Pierre Harrison (left) and two students, Sanpreet Kaur and Namita Alung, from her old school Tagore Baal Niketan. Standing behind them is a friend

living in the US, joined Bharatnatyam classes, attended Indian musical concerts and went to Indian restaurants. She gave Bharatnatyam performances and even taught her husband to cook popular Indian dishes like biryani!

After doing her Master of Science from the University of Texas in 1984, Kalpana joined the University of Colorado, Boulder, to do a PhD in aerospace under the guidance of Prof Don Wilson. The laboratory was her favourite haunt where she conducted several computer-modelling studies of various aircraft. Here, she was earning enough money for flying lessons at the local flying club. Earlier, in Karnal, she had wanted to join the local aviation club to become an amateur flyer like her brother but she needed the written permission of her father. Her father had flatly refused as he felt it was too risky for a young girl. Luckily in the US, she had no family restrictions to keep her passion for flying on leash. Moreover, she fell she should have experience of flying if she intended to design aeroplanes.

Harrison wholeheartedly supported her desire to fly. In fact, he himself began to give her flying lessons at the local flying club. They often flew together in gliders and aeroplanes and she secured various licences to become an instructor of flying single-and multiple-engine aeroplanes and even single-engine seaplanes. Her source of inspiration were several explorers and flyers but the first to inspire her was J R D Tata. During the two-week stint at the Aero Club of India, New Delhi, as a part of training of the Punjab Engineering College, she had seen the *Puss Moth* displayed there. Tata had flown this first commercial, single-seater plane from Karachi to Mumbai on October 15, 1932. Patty Wagstaff, the three times American aerobatics champion, was another aviator she admired. She herself learnt aerobatics and would do the rolls and loops during joyrides with her friends.

Colorado is a scenic place surrounded by mountains, rivers and forests, studded with hiking trails. It was an ideal spot for a sports-loving couple like Kalpana and

for the job. When she received the call letter from the NASA Astronaut Office in December 1994, she rang up Harrison, who was out of town, and left a message on voice mail. In her excitement she simply said, 'I'm in!' For some time Harrison could not understand what she meant and had to ring her back to check.

She was one of five women of a total 23 astronauts selected out of 2,962 applicants that year. She was also among seven non-Americans and the only civilian to be selected. She had to undergo a series of medical and psychological tests and interviews. During the process of selection, even a watch is kept on the behaviour of the applicants during their stay in the NASA hostels. Apart from qualifications and experience, the qualities that the NASA looks for in an astronaut are: character, integrity, intelligence, team spirit and even public speaking skills. She excelled in all these.

In March 1995, Kalpana joined the NASA Astronaut training camp at Johnson Space Center at Houston. It lasted for fourteen months and during the training, the participants are called 'Astronaut Candidates' (ASCANS). It is only after the completion of the rigorous training that the candidates are given the 'Astronaut' designation. The astronaut training consists of several parts. First, a theoretical knowledge of space flight, namely navigation and astronomy. Then, hands-on

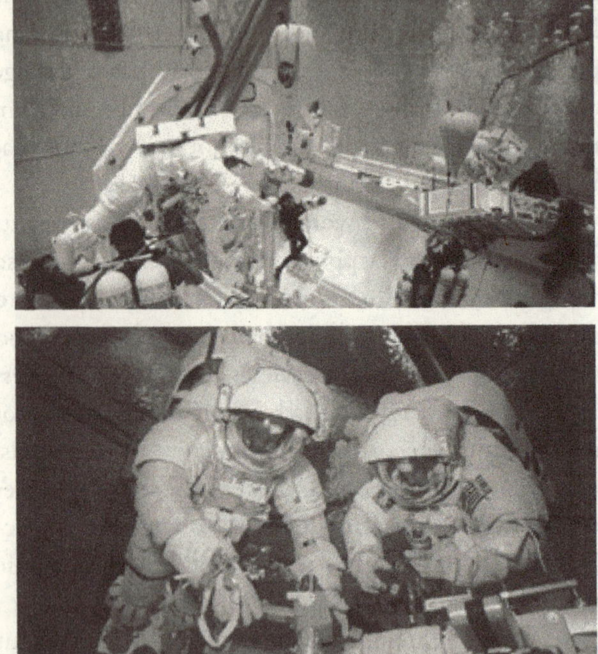

Undergoing training in specially simulated environments

experience with various systems of the Space Shuttle, their repair and maintenance; undergoing space-like conditions of vacuum and zero gravity in artificial simulators and even high altitude flying. Undergoing high acceleration conditions experienced during take-off in

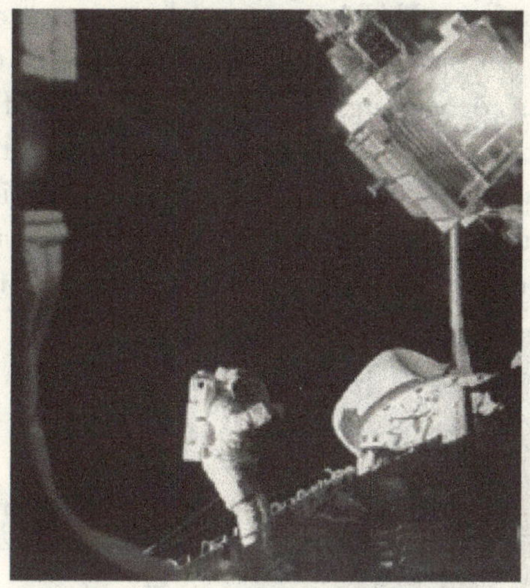

The satellite Spartan being released from the Payload Bay of Columbia during Kalpana's maiden space flight

flight simulators; training in the mock-ups of a Space Shuttle, practising various manoeuvres and undergoing emergency drills. Besides, the astronauts are also tested for their physical endurance, stamina and survival skills in a crisis. For instance, they are dropped into the sea, over mountains and jungles by boats or aeroplanes without food and water and have to find their way back on their own. Here, Kalpana's outdoor adventures with Harrison came in handy and she came through with flying colours.

Becoming a NASA astronaut does not guarantee a journey into space. That opportunity is offered to a few astronauts depending upon the requirements of a space mission. At the NASA Astronaut Office, astronauts perform many kinds of tasks—from looking into the feasibility of scientific experiments submitted for execution in space, to liaison with industries, laboratories, schools and colleges. They take classes, train astronauts and man the Houston Mission Control to share their experience and know how to deal with astronauts in trouble in space.

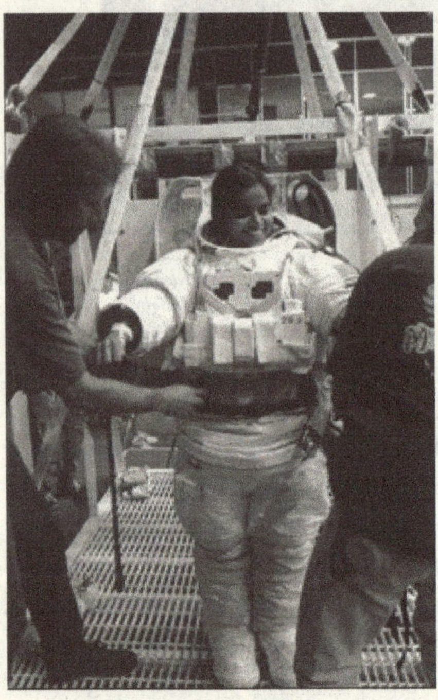

Donning the special suit and helmet

Moreover, every astronaut aboard a space mission has some

duties assigned to him. The Commander, often an ace aircraft pilot and experienced astronaut who has already been to space, is the overall incharge; he directs a space mission. The Pilot, again an ace aircraft pilot and experienced astronaut, has the duties of manoeuvring the shuttle in space and terrestrial atmosphere. The Mission Specialist, an astronaut with a technical background, coordinates the various activities of the shuttle, such as, checking and maintaining all its systems, conducting experiments, housekeeping and other miscellaneous tasks. The Payload Specialist is, on the other hand, a civilian technical expert specially trained for the space mission, who conducts specific

scientific experiments concerning the payload aboard the shuttle.

When on December 7, 1996, Kalpana received a phone call from the former Mission Specialist and astronaut David Leestma asking her if she was interested in working for him, she knew she had been selected for a space mission. Finally, her dream of a space flight would come true.

Kalpana had been selected for the Space Shuttle mission, called Space Transportation System-87, where 87

During her training programme

was the Flight tail number. It was called 'STS-87' in short. *Columbia*, named after the first American ship which circumvented the earth, was the shuttle selected for the mission. It was due to be launched in November 1997. She was selected as its Mission Specialist and Prime Robotic Arm Operator. After a lifetime of striving she knew she would become the first Indian woman in travel to space and her name would now be a part of Indian history. It had been a long journey from Karnal into outer space.

CHAPTER IV

THE MAIDEN SPACE FLIGHT

A Space Shuttle is a huge aeroplane-like spacecraft with one major difference. Instead of a passenger cabin, it has a cylindrical 'Payload Bay'. The Payload Bay, as the name implies, is the hold where payloads—equipment, satellites, materials, laboratories and even laboratory animals—to be carried for experimentation or launching into space are kept. Any manoeuvre or experiment to be performed in the bay can be controlled remotely from the cockpit. The upper curving doors of the bay can open or close in space as the situation demands.

The cockpit of a shuttle is similar to that of an aeroplane. Placed right at its nose, it is filled with windows, dials, buttons, communication links and control links and control levers. Here, two astronauts, the Commander and the Pilot, sit and manoeuvre it by firing its main engines and small thruster jets. These are placed at various points on its body, making it move like a glider while cruising through the terrestrial atmosphere. Just behind them sit two more astronauts, the Mission Specialists, who can if need be, assist them at any time. Just below the cockpit is another deck, called 'Mid-deck', where the other three astronauts, the Mission and Payload Specialists, sit. On this deck are also kept what are called 'Glove Boxes' containing equipment, instruments, laboratory animals, etc, needed for carrying out experiments in space.

Columbia on the launch pad. The rocket at the centre is the External Tank and those on the left and right sides are the Solid Boosters

The crew cabin where these astronauts live, eat and sleep in bunker-like beds is just below these decks. It is connected to the cockpit via a circular hatch. At the rear of the cockpit are two huge windows which look on the payload bay. The entire interior of the shuttle is designed to optimise its space for inclusion of miniaturised equipment required for travelling in space as well as for conducting experiments. It therefore always appears to be crammed with gizmos. It is the team spirit of every member of a mission, working in this weird-looking, claustrophobic interior of the shuttle, which is the key element in the success or failure of a space mission.

The astronauts aboard the shuttle are often divided into two teams. One team is mostly for manoeuvring in space and maintainence of the shuttle and the other for conducting experiments and keeping a watch over them. For the STS Mission-87, the Mission Commander was Kevin R. Kregel, Pilot Steven Lindsey, Mission Specialists Winston Scott, Takao Doi and Kalpana Chawla, and a Payload Specialist Leonid Kadenyuk. It was an international crew: Kregel, Lindsey and Scott were Americans, Doi was Japanese, Kadenyuk, a Ukrainian, and Kalpana an India-born American. While Kalpana was the second Indian—and the first Indian woman—to go into space, Doi was the first Japanese astronaut to do so.

For the launch into space, the shuttle is strapped to one huge external tank and two small booster rockets. To enter the shuttle, the astronauts have to climb to a height of 65 metres using a lift. They are all strapped to their seats, almost lying on their backs. As the countdown begins, all the various systems of the shuttle are checked one by one. At countdown zero, both the boosters are fired. With a huge blast of burnt fuel, which burns at the rate of 4,500 litres per second, the shuttle trembles as it slowly climbs up and then like a lightning streak disappears into the sky above.

After taking the shuttle to a predetermined altitude in about eight minutes, the two booster rockets become empty and fall back (in this case into the Atlantic Ocean), where they are recovered for re-fuelling and re-launch later. Meanwhile, the shuttle fires its main engines and using the fuel from the external tank rises higher into space. When this tank empties, the shuttle

Kalpana with the crew of her maiden space flight aboard Columbia

discards it too and, re-orients itself horizontally in space like an aeroplane, by firing two smaller engines and thruster jets. Thereafter called an 'Orbiter', it begins to orbit the earth like a satellite. It is then at an altitude of between 185 to 650 kilometres, moving at the hyper-sonic speed of 28,000 kilometres per hour around the earth situated at an angle to her equator.

As the Orbiter circles the earth, it slowly loses speed and therefore altitude. To maintain its orbiting altitude, the two small engines of the shuttle are fired off and on. For any other small manoeuvres in space, the thruster jets at various parts of its body are also fired regularly. After the completion of its mission in space,

Gearing up for her maiden space flight

the Orbiter is re-oriented to enter the terrestrial atmosphere, initially tail first. Its main engines are then fired from time to time—almost like putting brakes on the speed of the shuttle—to slow it down, so that it loses altitude. Finally, as it enters the atmosphere, it drifts down like a glider at an angle of 40 degrees in a series of S-shaped loops and lands on a specially made runaway on earth. Its entire machinery, components and computers are then checked, re-checked and its own fuel tanks re-fuelled for the next launch into space.

The toughest part of the shuttle flight are the initial eight minutes or so, when it is launched into space by the booster rockets. Moving against the gravitational pull of the earth, the speed of climb increases from zero to seven kilometres per second! For the astronauts in the shuttle, all hell breaks loose. While the loud, crackling noise of the burning fuel of the booster rockets is somewhat reduced by their padded helmets, their pulse-rates shoot up from 72 to 102 per minute within seconds! Besides, it feels as if a heavy load is pushing down on their chests and simultaneously the ceiling is pulling them up! Most of the training in flight simulators, where astronauts are exposed to extremely high accelerations, are to prepare them for this phase of the space flight.

However, once the boosters and the external tank have been discarded and the shuttle enters space, its orbit is stabilised and as it becomes an orbiter, astronauts heave a sigh of relief. They then enter the next and far easier phase of the space flight. They remove their heavy space-suits and change into comfortable clothing. The pressure inside the shuttle is maintained at the normal atmospheric pressure that exists on the terrestrial surface. The doors of the Payload Bay are then opened to let out the heat that accumulates in the shuttle during takeoff. In the initial few days in space, astronauts feel disorientated and are unable to sleep properly. Their faces also become bloated as water roams freely in their bodies.

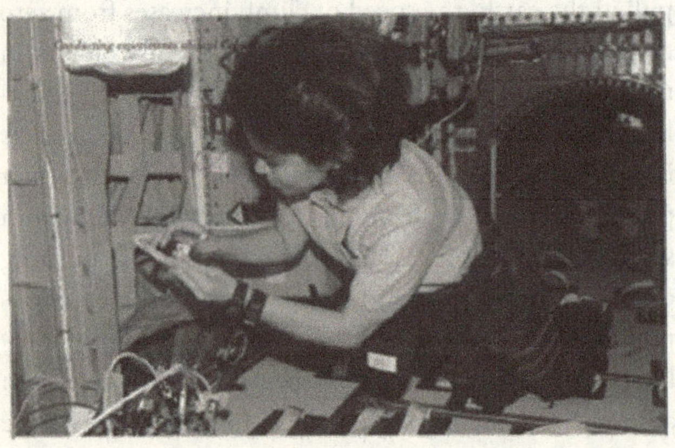

Conducting experiments aboard Columbia

Walking in space is almost like floating in a swimming pool and astronauts are trained for that on earth. The absence of gravity magnifies all movements several times causing them to tumble over at the slightest gesture. Any object placed at a point in space continues to remain there unless and until it is moved. Astronauts therefore, have to be extremely careful in performing any task, whether it is walking, handling gadgets, wearing a dress or eating. All food, materials and gadgets are specially designed and packed taking into account these conditions. The food is similar to camp food—dehydrated and sealed in foil packages.

The entire flight schedule of the shuttle is planned much in advance by the Mission Managers. Every waking minute of all astronauts and every manoeuvre of the shuttle for conducting experiments and exploration are planned in detail. In fact, astronauts are trained for the experiments and exploration they are to conduct inside and outside the shuttle with rigorous hands-on sessions with all the equipment and instruments.

All the manoeuvres and space walks of the astronauts outside the shuttle, called 'Extra Vehicular Activities' (EVAs) are also tried and tested several times in simulation chambers. If some changes in schedule occur at any time, even those manoeuvres are first tried in simulation chambers and then astronauts are given the green signal to carry them out in real space conditions! It is only in an emergency that astronauts are allowed to take their own decisions. Every time astronauts conduct a space walk or test a novel gadget or conduct an experiment in space, they have to write a report immediately. These reports are eventually submitted to Mission Control on their return to earth. These reports will come in handy during future space exploration, for instance, in building the International Space Station in the coming decades.

As the Orbiter is at an altitude from where the sun is visible round the clock, there is no day or night for astronauts. Often, day and night are kept in tune with their biological clocks. In other words, their day and

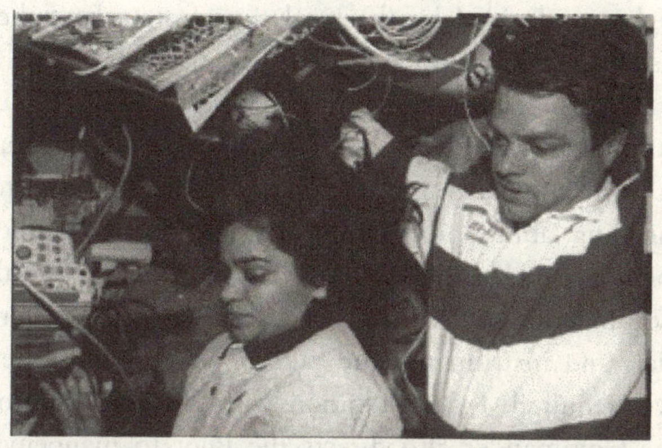

Kalpana with the crew of her maiden space flight aboard Columbia

night are decided by the local time from where they have been launched.

A day in the life of an astronaut aboard a shuttle runs something like this: They are woken up by a wake-up call which is a favourite song of one of them. Then after morning ablutions, exercise and breakfast together, their planned duties for the day begin. The Shuttle Commander and Mission Specialists check all meters, dials and instruments and take down readings wherever required. In consultation with Mission Control, the Commander also directs the Pilot to manoeuvre the shuttle in space, to ensure the desired attitude and orbiting speed. Thereafter all go for their scheduled tasks. Meanwhile, the Mission and Payload Specialists

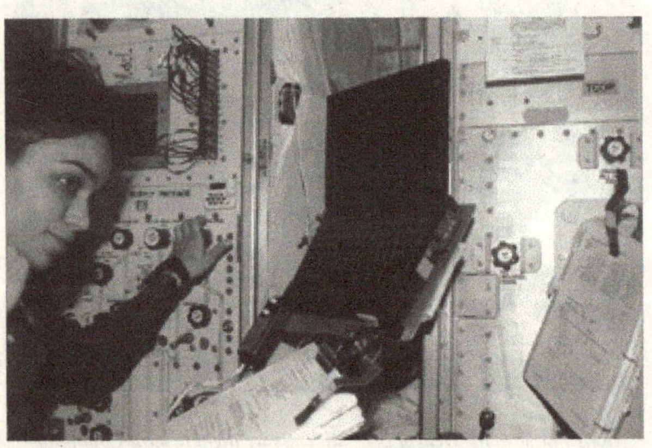

visit the Mid-deck, conduct and watch the experiments in progress in the Glove Boxes, take down readings or start new experiments. If some experiments are in progress in the Payload Bay, they are watched from the cockpit and controlled remotely.

While these mission activities are in progress, astronauts also get the opportunity to talk with their families, important visitors or participate in 'Press Conferences' with the media through video-teleconferences, send e-mails, sometimes discuss experiments and problems with the concerned scientists or school students on earth. In other words, the Orbiter functions like any other laboratory on the surface of the earth. The working day, often of sixteen hours, is filled with activities and then they sleep for eight hours in the crew cabin below the cockpit.

It was about seven hours after the launch on November 19, 1997, that *Columbia* crossed over the Indian subcontinent. The reason for this delay was the inclination of the orbit of the shuttle—about 29 degree—to the equator of the earth. On every orbit around the earth, only a narrow strip of land below can be clearly seen from the shuttle. With considerable joy and thrill, Kalpana pointed out her hometown Karnal to her fellow-astronauts. Throughout the flight she took breathtaking photographs of the earth for studies later.

In fact, the earth was her special concern and she always looked at it with love and affection from her window before she went to sleep every 'day'.

Her sensitive description of the earth uttered during the space flight have today become immortal. On one occasion, she remarked, 'This planet below you is our campsite, and you know of no other campground.' On December 3, 1998, she had a telephonic conversation with the then Prime Minister of India, I K Gujral, who congratulated her on the pioneering space feat and strengthening US-India relations. The US President Bill Clinton also had a video conference with all the astronauts. 'Your smiles made my day,' he said from Camp David, 'I look forward to seeing you back here on earth.'

During the space flight. Kalpana and other astronauts conducted science experiments in the Glove Boxes to test the effect of zero gravity and vacuum conditions of space on various phenomena not yet properly understood on earth. It is possible to create a near vacuum on earth but its gravity cannot be switched off. Experiments have therefore to be performed in space to ascertain the effect of zero gravity on various phenomena. For instance, Kalpana conducted experiments to observe how stronger alloys could be made by studying the way two metals mix, how better silicon chips could be made by observing the way silica material solidifies, how better engines could be designed for aeronautical and industrial purposes by understanding what makes flames stable and emit less pollutants.

The Ukrainian astronaut Kadenvuk monitored the behaviour of a colony of ants and the growth of plants of soyabean and mustard from seeds under space conditions. The project on ant behaviour was with some Ukrainian and American school students. So occasionally, he talked with the concerned teachers and students. Meanwhile, Steven Lindsay monitored the ozone layer, the atmospheric layer which prevents harmful radiations of the sun from reaching the earth.

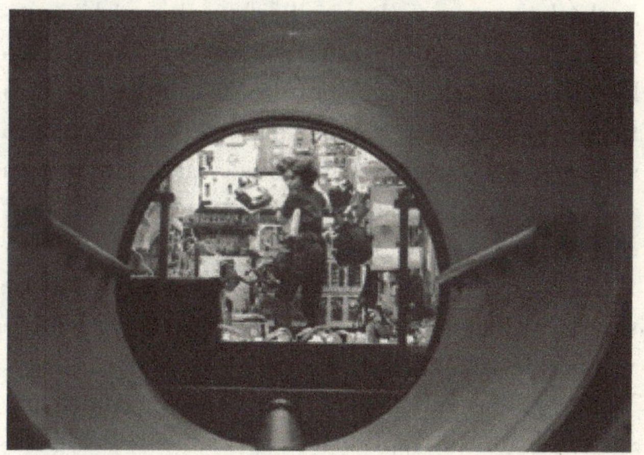

Busy with scientific experiments in zero-gravity environment aboard Columbia

Other astronauts left the shuttle on several occasions, took space walks and conducted tests on equipment. The equipment included a six-metre long manually operated crane and a radio-controlled, free flying video camera, the size of a beach ball. They are likely to be used during the construction of the International Space Station, called 'Freedom'. Throughout the space flight, Kalpana also monitored all computer software that controlled the functioning of the shuttle.

One of her primary tasks was to operate the sixteen-metre long robotic arm of the Payload Bay to pick up the satellite *Spartan* from its hold in the bay and release it into space. This satellite was supposed to study the stream of electrically charged particles coming from the sun, called, 'solar wind', and the crown-like outermost atmosphere the 'corona' of the sun. It so happened that when Kalpana released the satellite into space using the robotic arm, it slipped and spun in such a manner that it could not be re-oriented for the study of the sun.

After consultation with the Mission Control, the shuttle was manoeuvred some days later for a rendezvous with the satellite. Commander Kevin Kregel, Winston Scott and Takao Doi were then sent out into space to manually capture the expensive satellite hovering nearby, latch it into the hold of the Payload Bay and bring it back to earth. Later, ground investigations revealed that the *Spartan* could not be released correctly by Kalpana not because she had mishandled it but due to an inbuilt fault in its working mechanism. The NASA authorities subsequently declared that there was no negligence on her part and declared her to be a 'terrific astronaut'. The very fact they went on to select her for a second space mission later showed their confidence in her abilities.

Earlier, during her first space flight Kalpana had the presence of mind to take forty photographs of the external tank within two and a half minutes during take off, when all astronauts are mentally and physically disoriented! The photos showed for the first time how fuel vents from the tank during those final minutes of the shuttle's climb into space.

On December 5, 1997, the shuttle was manoeuvred to return to earth. Floating like a glider, it entered the terrestrial atmosphere and landed on the runaway of the Kennedy Space Center. All the families of the astronauts, including Kalpana's, were eagerly waiting to meet them at the Center. And, they all said a prayer of thanks when the shuttle made a safe touchdown.

After quarantine procedures, when astronauts are thoroughly checked for any harmful alien microbe on or in their bodies, they familiarise themselves with the gravity of the earth, take rest and sleep. Then they are allowed to meet their relatives. It was a moment of great pride for the entire Chawla family as Kalpana became the first Indian woman to go into space. She stayed in space for about 376 hours and 34 minutes, orbited the earth 252 times and covered a distance of 14.3 million kilometres—much more than what Sally Ride, the first American woman astronaut, did during her maiden space flight. It was an extraordinary achievement for a girl from Karnal and all of India rejoiced at her triumph.

CHAPTER V

THE FINAL ODYSSEY

Her successful maiden flight made Kalpana a celebrity all over the word, especially in India and the US. Although the Russian, Valentina Tereshkova was the first woman to go into space as long ago as 1963, Kalpana's feat is no mean achievement. She was the first Indian and Asian woman astronaut to travel in space. But this new status did not affect her behaviour at all. She was as modest and humble as ever and led a quiet life. If she met somebody on a street corner or market, she never introduced herself as an astronaut but said simply, 'Hi! I'm Kalpana Chawla!' Despite all the publicity about the STS-87 space flight in the media, she would still meet people at flying clubs who asked her whether she could fly an aeroplane, and she would sweetly respond, 'Fly with me and see for yourself!' She was like a typical girl next-door and her neighbours always found her cheerful, courteous and helpful. Her house was decorated in a traditional Indian style, filled with Rajasthani handicrafts and knick-knacks. She was often seen jogging with her husband, going for swimming or busy with the potted plants in the garden of her house. Only her old car carried the sticker 'Space is our future'.

Kalpana was often invited to schools and colleges to address students and share with them her experiences in space. Talking directly and with humour she always encouraged students to dream big and 'follow their dream'. During interactive sessions in schools, she urged students to take up science and mathematics because they are the foundations of modern civilisation. Supporting her talk with slide shows on her space trip, she always emphasised that the earth was a very precious planet and we should do all we can to save it from destruction.

Kalpana had also become very popular in the Indian community settled in the United States. Often referred to as 'Miss India' as she was the most conspicuous Indian woman in that country, she participated in various Indian functions and festivals celebrated there. In spite of her fame she did not lose touch with her family, teachers and friends back in India. In fact, even before the maiden space flight, she made special efforts to renew contact with her old school and college teachers in Karnal and Chandigarh and kept in touch with them by telephone and e-mail and on her maiden space trip, she took with her the logos and mementos of her old school and college, both in India and the US along with her family photos.

Her teachers and the students of her school also reciprocated her affectionate gesture. On the eve of her maiden space flight, all the students wore a specially designed T-shirt bearing the logo 'Tagoreans Are Proud of Kalpana' and marched from the school to the neighbouring Karna Stadium, where the elite of Karnal had gathered to mark the historic event. The house where she was born—now re-built into a palatial bungalow—was also decorated on that day with colourful lights and the owner of the house, Vijay Sethia, a relative of Kalpana, distributed sweets to mark the historic event.

On her return from space, she was also keen to visit India but due to fears of terrorism in the subcontinent, the US Government refused her permission to do so. Kalpana began to ensure that every year two students from Tagore Baal Niketan could visit the International

Space School Foundation at Houston. Here, school students from all over the world are invited to see space training facilities and learn about space exploration first hand from astronauts and space experts. This is part of the preparations for the International Space Station, which NASA is presently assembling in space.

The students from India were Kalpana's special guests. Often, she and Harrison invited them to their house during weekends. While Kalpana chatted with them, and recalled with nostalgia her days spent at Karnal, Harrison would prepare biryani for them! In her old school, she soon became popular as Kalpana Didi.

Teachers and students of the Punjab Engineering College, Chandigarh, posing with the specially prepared memento

Normally, any astronaut who has gone to space once is not too keen to enter it again, as by this time, he is fully aware of the hazards involved in space flights. But Kalpana was not the one to feel her job was over and that she should now enjoy her celebrity status. She was keen to go to space again. Often, she said she would like to be part of the first team that landed on the planet Mars, where NASA plans to set up a base in the coming decades. She was even ready to join the team going to the Red Planet whose return was not guaranteed! In fact, she always expressed the wish that she would prefer to die in space among the stars.

The NASA astronauts are not free to simply enjoy their celebrity status once they are back on earth. They all have to work in the NASA Astronaut Office at Houston. Of course, most astronauts opt out of active service, some join Mission Control in an advisory capacity, others take up bureaucratic work involving liaison with industries, laboratories, schools and colleges and some join the training programmes. After her return to the NASA Astronaut Office, Kalpana also excelled in her ground duties. NASA gave her a special award for doing the work of two persons simultaneously in two completely different areas.

However, only a few astronauts keep open the option of going again into space and Kalpana was one.

So, one day when she received a telephone call from a Mission In-charge asking her about the tasks she was busy with, she gave all the details. However, when the In-charge wondered whether she would still have time for another space mission, she was surprised and delighted and agreed immediately. She was selected as a Flight Engineer and Mission Specialist for her second and last space flight. Now, she finally had the designation of 'Flight Engineer' which was her long-cherished childhood ambition!

The Space Shuttle STS-87 Mission—Kalpana's first space flight—was more or less for gaining experience in manoeuvering men and equipment in space. It was a part of the preparations for the construction of the International Space Station. On the other hand, the Space Shuttle STS-107 Mission – Kalpana's

The seven member crew of the Space Shuttle Mission STS-107 during a press briefing before a launch into space

second – was a purely scientific mission. All the astronauts even participated in some medical experiments conducted on their own bodies! There was an all inclusive laboratory called 'Spacehab'—about 7 metres long, 5 metres wide and 4 metres high—containing furnaces, instruments, test-tubes, cameras and computers. It was maintained at the atmospheric pressure required for scientific experiments and was specially built and installed inside the Payload Bay of the shuttle. It was connected directly to the Mid-deck of the shuttle through a tunnel. Incidently, the 23-year old *Columbia* was again selected for the STS-107 Mission.

This second space mission was delayed by several months as the shuttle underwent checks and re-checks. There was also an eleventh hour delay in the launch as even after donning their space-suits all astronauts had to wait for three hours before they could enter the

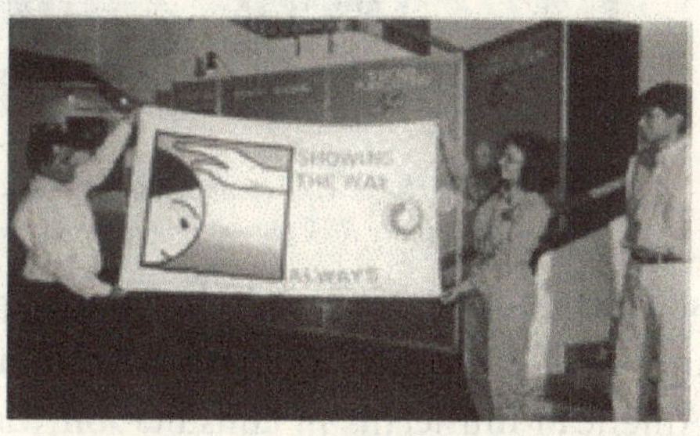

A S Manekar, Director, National Science Center, New Delhi, handing over a specially made banner to Sunita Choudhary, the eldest sister of Kalpana before Kalpana's second space flight

The crew of STS-107 waving goodbye just before boarding Columbia. Commander Rick Husband is at the extreme right

shuttle! For this mission, Kalpana had specially selected music CDs of Abida Parveen, Ravi Shankar and some American musicians in consultation with Harrison for the morning wake-up call. She was also carrying specially designed mementos from her school, engineering college, National Science Centre, Nehru Planetarium, and the Aero Club of India. She also carried a white silk banner dedicated to her teachers. It had picture of a girl bowing before her teacher.

On this mission Kalpana's companion astronauts were Commander Rick Husband, Pilot William McCool, Mission Specialists Laurel Clark and David Brown, and Payload Commander Michael Anderson, who were all Americans. The Payload Specialist was Iian Ramon who was the first Israeli astronaut to go into space. Due to the fear of a terrorist attack against Ramon this particular mission had considerably tighter security.

During the launch of the *Columbia* on January 16, 2003, some material – some claim 'foam' and others 'snowball' from the external tank – was observed to have fallen on the tile-covered wing of the shuttle causing a minor crack. But at that juncture, when the boosters had been fired and there was no way to stop them, this incident was ignored. The crack was felt to be of no great danger to the safety of the shuttle. As the subsequent events showed, it proved to be the cause of the fatal accident. Nevertheless, the shuttle was safely placed in an orbit of the earth at the altitude of 274 kilometres for the next 15 days at an angle of 39 degree to the equator of the earth.

During the entire mission, eighty scientific experiments were conducted aboard the shuttle, of which Kalpana was exclusively responsible for performing twelve. Again, the purpose of the experiments was observing how living beings, materials and other phenomena, behave in the absence of the disturbing effect of the earth's gravity and atmosphere. For instance, though an ordinary candle flame is the commonest phenomenon on the earth, about 150 chemical reactions occur in it. These reactions are still not clearly understood due to the convection currents set up by the earth's gravity and air. In fact, a candle flame does not have a drop-like but a spherical shape in space.

Using the sophisticated facilities available in the Spacehab, Kalpana studied the chemical reactions occurring in a candle flame, how it produces soot and other emissions, including pollutants, so that it could be optimally harnessed for mankind, for fire is the driving force of all engines and industrial plants. Her studies would directly benefit the fabrication of more effective engines especially for aircraft and industries. She also studied how fire could effectively be brought under control and extinguished especially in closed spaces, such as, libraries, aircraft, ships and spacecraft, using the cheaper water mist sprays. This could lead to the development of a new fire-fighting technique. It would replace the present ones that use harmful chemicals, such as, halons, which damage the ozone layer.

These main experiments apart, Kalpana also conducted experiments to create in space conditions, new pure and flawless alloys, silicon chips, crystals and proteins. She grew different types of cell cultures which would give insights into fighting prostrate cancer and improving crop yield. She also studied how granular structures compress together, which would help in building stronger foundations for buildings in areas prone to earthquakes, floods and tornadoes.

Kalpana also lent a helping hand in other experiments in progress aboard the shuttle, namely, observing the behaviour of giant ants, fish, spiders, bees, silkworms and rodents, and the blooming of roses and rice flowers. These interesting experiments, which were selected by NASA after considerable review, were submitted by school students from Australia, China, Israel,

Japan and USA. Besides, all the astronauts were guinea pigs for medical experiments. As soon as the Orbiter had stabilised in space, they swallowed calcium tracers. The effect of weightlessness on the functioning of various body systems, namely, cardiovascular, cardiopulmonary, musculoskeletal and immune, was observed during their stay in space. As Flight Engineer for the mission, Kalpana's duties included checking the functioning of all systems aboard the shuttle in a systematic manner, diagnose any malfunction and rectify it. On occasions, she also had to assist the Commander in various navigational tasks.

Aboard the Columbia during its orbital flight

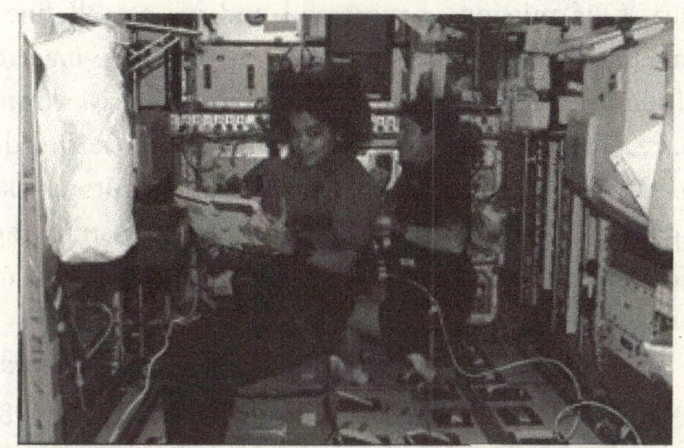

Kalpana conducted all the experiments successfully except for the failure of one furnace soon after the shuttle entered space. She switched on a video camera so people on earth could see what she was doing and she transmitted the results to Mission Control as the experiments progressed. Today, it is claimed that between 50 to 90% of the data about the experiments has been safely received at Mission Control and is being analysed.

Meanwhile, the Israeli astronaut had a talk with the Israeli President and his family members. He also interacted with the Israeli media. The astronauts had a short interactive session with the US President George Bush and the three American astronauts who were then aboard the International Space Station in the assembly stage. The last message to be received from the shuttle was: 'Our mission is successful and we are all fine'. Kalpana also sent what proved to be her last e-mail to a friend marvelling at the beauty of the Nile river from space. The last video scene transmitted by the shuttle to Mission Control showed all the astronauts cracking jokes and teasing each other and happily strapping themselves to their seats to prepare for their return to earth.

In the early morning hours of February 1, 2003, just sixteen minutes before the scheduled landing, *Columbia* broke apart into two pieces over the state of Texas and all seven astronauts met a fiery death. Their charred bodies were later recovered among the debris of the shuttle scattered over the states of Texas and Florida. It was a tragic and heartbreaking end to a heroic career.

The debris from Columbia being studied to identify the cause of the disaster

Kalpana died where she had wished to end her life—in space. Her body was cremated and as she had wanted, the ashes were scattered across the National Park at Utah and over the Himalayas.

CHAPTER VI

DAUGHTER OF THE SOIL

'This may sound funny, but when I settle down I hope to live in a colony on Mars,' replied Kalpana once to a question raised by a journalist. Indeed, from childhood her eyes were always trained at the stars, which is where she found her final home. Although born in a small provincial town of India, where even today human-driven cycle-rickshaws outnumber motorised vehicles and the birth of a girl is not always a welcome event, she believed herself to be a citizen of the world and was always free from all prejudices of caste, race and religion. And despite the fact that she married a French-American and went into space aboard an American spacecraft, she lived like an Indian.

Shortish – about five feet – and dark-eyed, Kalpana's spoken English was free from an American accent or slangs. She enjoyed Indian musical concerts and Bharatnatyam performances, was a vegetarian and went to Indian restaurants in America to eat her favourite *samosa* with *imli-chutney* and *sev-puri.* Once, when she came to know that her favourite fries marketed by a popular American fast-food chain contained beef tallow oil she gave up eating them! In space she only ate raisins, nuts, cornflakes, bread cookies and drank tea. Even during the celebration of Thanksgiving aboard *Columbia* on the second space flight, she ate vegetarian food, while the others ate turkey. Her house was also furnished in a traditional Indian style and decorated with Indian handicrafts.

Kalpana was extremely proud of her birth-place and made every effort to bring it into the limelight. During space flights she would proudly point it out to her fellow-astronauts. Once, during the second space flight she remembered her closest friend, Daisy Chawla, who died in a

road accident. In fact, despite her celebrity status, she took pains to track down her former teachers, classmates and friends in India and showed a keen desire to stay in touch with them. Her affectionate and humble nature won the hearts of all who came in contact with her.

Although Kalpana was brought up in a religious environment, she never practised any religion. She was secular at heart, was deeply spiritual and loved listening to *bhajans* and *kirtans.* She was especially fond of Sufi music. Later, in the US, she discovered some western musicians, whose music she felt was deeply spiritual. In fact, if she was religious about anything it was about flying! Flying appealed to all her senses, whereas the theoretical side challenged her mind.

Thoughtful and philosophical by temperament, Kalpana was fond of reading especially literature, stories of adventure and exploration, and spiritual journeys. Her role models were several pilots, explorers and astronauts, like J R D Tata, Charles Lindbergh, Patty Wagstaff, Ernest Shackleton, Michael Collins and John Young. The spiritual journeys of Peter Matthiessen who wrote about his treks on foot across the Himalayas and African continent inspired her and she loved the writings of the environmentalist Carl Safina. The crucial element of her success was perseverance in face of all odds while reading and exploration broadened her perspective and outlook on life and enriched the journey to her goal.

Kalpana always loved and enjoyed her work. She was always highly attentive to the task before her, whether it was a classroom lecture or the performance of an experiment aboard the shuttle. Even during briefings to astronauts, while others simply listened, she always took notes. Above all, she possessed this inner striving to do something extraordinary in life. She always urged young people to take time to figure out what they wanted to do in life and what they enjoyed doing. And once that is done, she urged them to strive hard to achieve that goal. She always believed the journey to be as important as the goal.

Although Kalpana had a strong desire to go to Mars, fly over its canyons and die in space, she was equally concerned about the well-being of the earth. She always urged young people to listen to the sounds of nature and take care of our fragile planet. During her space trips, she took many breathtaking photographs of the earth for various terrestrial studies later on the ground. When she was in space, she always felt a sense of connection with everyone on earth.

It was Kalpana's cherished desire to visit India again. But that was not to be. A few months after her tragic death, Harrison visited India. He went to her school and college, met her family, teachers and friends and scattered her ashes over the Himalayas.

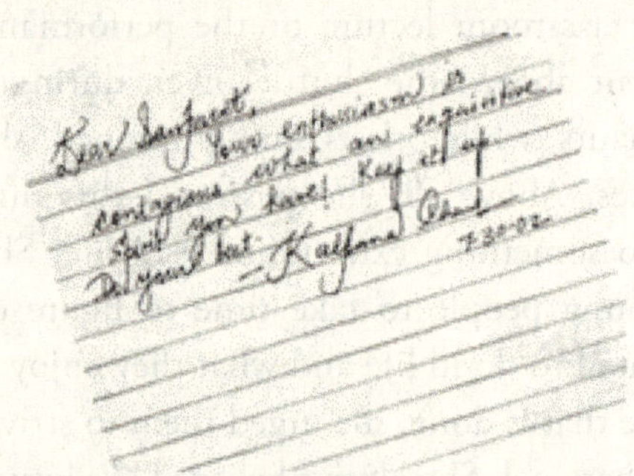

Dear Sanpreet,
Your enthusiasm is
contagious. What an inquisitive
spirit you have! Keep it up.
Do your best.
—Kalpana Chawla
7-30-02

Kalpana's message to Sanpreet Kaur, a student from her former school

SAYINGS OF KALPANA CHAWLA

- Follow your dreams.
- The path from dreams to reality does exist. May you have the vision to find it, the courage to get onto it and the perserverance to follow it. *(This is the last message e-mailed to the students of Punjab Engineering College, Chandigarh, from the Space Shuttle.)*
- The quickest way may not necessarily be the best.
- Enjoying what you are doing now is the most important thing.
- You must enjoy the journey, because whether or not you get there, you really must have fun on the way.
- The astronaut's job requires a technical background and a strong desire ... to go out in the blue yonder.
- Pioneers don't have role models.
- I was overwhelmed most by the sense that it took only 90 minutes to circle the planet. Just 90 minutes. Even though I had known that, it was an overpowering sensation to know how small this place is.
- ...In the retina of my eye, the whole earth and the sky would be seen reflected ... and everybody said: 'Oh! Wow!'

CHRONOLOGY

1962	Born on March 17 (official July 1, 1961), Karnal, Haryana.
1976	Passed Class X, Tagore Baal Niketan School, Karnal.
1977	Passed Pre-University, DAV College for Women, Karnal.
1978	Passed Pre-Engineering, Dyal Singh College, Karnal.
1982	BSc in aeronautical engineering, Punjab Engineering College, Chandigarh, stands third in her class. Leaves for the US.
1983	December 2, marries Jean Pierre Harrison.
1984	Master of Science (MS) in aerospace engineering, University of Texas, Arlington.
1988	PhD in aerospace engineering, University of Colorado, Boulder; hired by MCAT Institute, California, as a Research Scientist for NASA Ames Research Center, California.

1993	Joined as Research Scientist and Vice President, Overset Methods Inc, California.
1994	Selected by the National Aeronautics and Space Administration (NASA) as Astronaut.
1995	March, joined the Johnson Space Center, Houston, for astronaut training programme.
1997	First space flight as a Mission Specialist aboard Space Shuttle Columbia on Mission STS-87 which was launched on November 19 and returned to earth on December 5 after logging about 376 hours in space; she was the Prime Robotic Operator for the mission.
2003	Selected as a Flight Engineer and Mission Specialist aboard Space Shuttle Columbia on Mission STS-107; launched on January 16. Died aboard it on February 1, when it exploded in the atmosphere at an altitude of 63 kilometres and about 16 minutes before its scheduled landing at Kennedy Space Centre runway.

The total time Kalpana Chawla spent in space was: 31 days, 14 hours and 54 minutes.

ACKNOWLEDGEMENTS

Although a large amount of material on the life and contributions of Kalpana Chawla was available on the internet, I was not sure about its authenticity. I, therefore, decided to check all the facts. I visited Karnal and Chandigarh to talk to her teachers, friends, colleagues and relatives. My hunch was correct, there were several mistakes in the various websites, magazines and newspapers. For instance, she was not a Sikh, she never lived in the Himgiri hostel of the Punjab Engineering College and she did not stand first in the engineering degree.

The following persons have been very helpful in gathering the correct facts but I must add that if there are any errors in the book they are mine: Amarjeet Kohli, Prof V S Malhotra, Prof S C Sharma, Prof Uma Batra, Vimala Raheja, Daljit K Madan, Raminder Kaur, Verinder Kaur, Dr Renu Mittal, K K Bansal, Deepak Majumdar, Sanpreet Kaur and Namita Alung.

I am also thankful to the following persons/organisations for the photographs published in the book: Asok Samanta, American Center, New Delhi; Ajit Mehta, Mehta Photo Studio, Karnal; Prof V S Malhotra and Prof S C Sharma, Punjab Engineering College, Chandigarh; A S Manekar, Director, National Science Centre, New Delhi; Daljit K Madan and Sanpreet Kaur, Tagore Baal Niketan Senior Secondary School; Dr Renu Mittal, Panipat; and NASA. I am also grateful to a member of Kalpana's family, who wants to remain anonymous, for going through this book and correcting some errors that were widely reported in various media. As a result, a reader may find this book differing in some facts from the other books published on Kalpana. All I can add is that I have tried my best to make this biography as authentic as possible.